God's Little Flower

The Story of St. Thérèse of Lisieux

By
Chris Driscoll

Illustrated by
Patrick Kelley

Ambassador Books, Inc. • Worcester, Massachusetts

Also written by Chris Driscoll:

And God Blessed the Irish — The Story of Patrick

ISBN: 1-929039-05-0
Library of Congress Control Card Number: 2001087301

Published in the United States by Ambassador Books, Inc.
71 Elm Street, Worcester, Massachusetts 01609
(800) 577-0909

Printed in Canada.

For current information about all titles from Ambassador Books, Inc. visit our website at:
www.ambassadorbooks.com

To all of
God's little flowers.

The world was in a bad mood. Children cried. Dogs barked. It rained. The wind was cold and sharp. And people with sad faces walked down the street.

Parents worried about their children. And children complained about their parents. Families never seemed to have quite enough money. And children always wanted more toys.

The newspapers said things were bad. There were earthquakes and wars. People were starving in India. And in Africa, many people were sick with diseases.

It was just like today. Everyone wanted to be happy, but almost no one was. People knew they lacked something in their lives, but they did not know what they were missing.

Of course, there were exceptions—one was a little girl named Thérèse who lived in France and who loved flowers and who found the secret to happiness.

Thérèse was not perfect. She was proud and impatient and stubborn and sensitive. And sometimes things happened that made her angry, and sometimes she pouted and sometimes she cried.

She had many reasons to be sad. She was often ill, and when she caught a cold she would become very sick, much sicker than most children.

And when she was only four something happened that seemed to put a dark cloud over her life.

Her mother, who loved her very much, died.

When Thérèse was ten years old she became very sick. She perspired from a high fever and shook with chills, and even became delirious.

Doctors were called to her home. But they were puzzled by Thérèse's illness. Her sickness went on week after week.

Her father and her sisters felt helpless. It seemed that nothing on earth could help her. The house was filled with sadness and there seemed to be nowhere to turn.

But then Thérèse prayed to the Blessed Mother with all her heart.

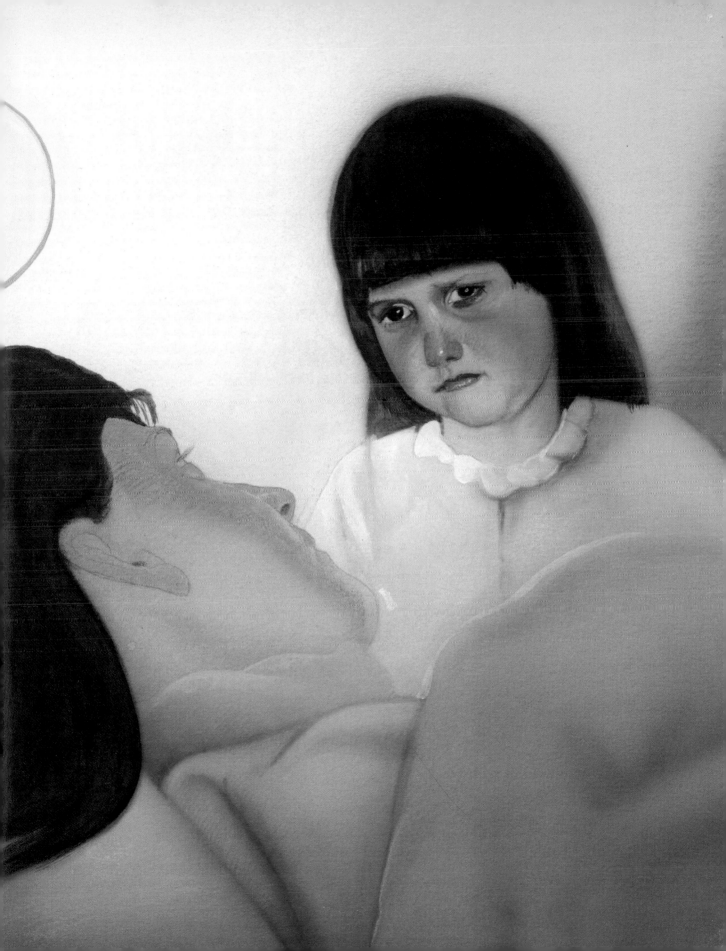

And suddenly, she saw a beautiful woman standing in front of her. It was the Mother of Jesus, and she was smiling at Thérèse. Her smile seemed to reach right to Thérèse's soul, and as it did, Thérèse was healed.

Thérèse's older sister, Leonie, decided one day that she was too old to play with dolls. So she brought a basket filled with doll clothes to her younger sisters, Celine and Thérèse.

"Choose what you want," Leonie said to the two little girls.

Celine looked carefully and picked out a pretty ball of wool, but Thérèse said, "I choose all." She took the whole basket.

And no one was surprised, and no one dared to say a word because Thérèse was very, very sensitive.

Thérèse always knew the most important thing that anyone can ever know. Thérèse knew that Jesus loved her.

And there was something else. Ever since she could remember, Thérèse knew that she loved God, and that she should love everybody else, too.

But it's not easy to love. Sometimes people are mean or silly or tired or angry, and sometimes they don't love us.

And Thérèse knew it was much easier to cry or pout or stamp her foot than to love someone who upset her.

She was just so little, and her love was so little, that she was not strong enough or big enough to really, really love.

How can I love when I get sick?
Or when I don't get what I want?
How can I love when it's raining out?
And people are mean and I am sad?
How can I love so that my love helps those
who cannot love?
How can I love so that my love changes the
lives of unhappy people?
I can't do that because I am too small.
I can't do that because I am too weak.
I can't do that because I am only Thérèse.
I can't do that because I am only a little child.

Thérèse loved the garden. She loved flowers. She loved sunlight. She loved to see things grow.

And one day she found a poor little flower that was very weak because it was always in the shade.

So Thérèse moved the flower. She took it out of the shade and planted it in the sunshine where it could be warm and healthy.

And each day, the little flower got stronger. And each day, the little flower grew. And each day, the little flower became more beautiful.

Thérèse knew that it was the warmth of God's love that made the flower grow.

And as Thérèse thought about the flower, she realized that she was like the flower. The warmth of God's love was giving her life and making her grow, too.

And then a thought came to her like a beam of light and brightened her soul. "I am God's little flower," she thought.

But even God's Little Flower had bad days when she was angry or disappointed or upset.

Sometimes people hurt her without meaning to. Sometimes people were mean to her just because they were mean people.

But God loves people even if they are mean. And Thérèse knew that she should love them, too.

How can I love when I get sick?
Or when I don't get what I want?
How can I love when it's raining out?
And people are mean and I am sad?
How can I love so that my love helps those
who cannot love?
How can I love so that my love changes the
lives of unhappy people?
I can't do that because I am too small.
I can't do that because I am too weak.
I can't do that because I am only Thérèse.
I can't do that because I am only a little child.

Then one Christmas everything changed. And all at once Thérèse really understood what it means to be loved by Jesus.

Thérèse would cry about almost anything—because her feelings were hurt, or because she thought someone else's feelings were hurt.

She could not help it. She was just very, very sensitive. So most of the time her family was very careful not to make her cry.

Sensitive people can be even more sensitive at Christmas time.

We expect everything to be perfect and when it is not, we get very, very sad and very, very upset. We don't want to be that way. We just are. And that's the way Thérèse was, too, until that special Christmas when she was almost fourteen.

As she and her family came home from Midnight Mass, Thérèse was very happy. It was time to open her presents. But her father was tired and grouchy. He was not in the mood to celebrate. In fact, he grumbled and said, "This will be the last year for presents."

Thérèse ran upstairs and tears filled her eyes. Her Christmas was ruined. Her joy was stolen away.

And then something wonderful happened. At one moment, she was sad and full of self-pity. At the next, she was filled with joy.

It was Christmas, and Jesus loved her. And his love filled her and spilled out of her and filled the house.

She ran downstairs and began to open her presents, to the great delight of her father.

There is a mystery to life and goodness, which only God can explain.

Some people work all their lives and gain nothing but money. Others are touched by the finger of God, and his love rushes out of them to shine in a dark and dangerous world.

On that Christmas morning, Jesus was born in Thérèse. His love became her love, and her love became his. His life became her life and her life became his.

In the time it takes to go up a stair, Thérèse was transformed.

Now can I love, so that my love helps those
who cannot love?
Now can I love, so that my love changes the
lives of unhappy people?
Or am I too small and too weak?

There was a criminal named Pranzini who was sentenced to death for his crimes.

Pranzini was a hard, cold man who turned away from love. He was lost and far from God. Thérèse had never seen him, but she loved him and prayed for him.

The world believed that Pranzini would die angry and unforgiven. But Thérèse knew that was not true. She asked God to give her a sign so that she could know that her love and her prayers had the power of Jesus.

After Pranzini was executed, the newspapers reported that just before he was put to death he suddenly turned and took a crucifix from a priest and kissed the wounds of Jesus three times.

And Thérèse knew that her prayers had the power of Jesus. Pranzini, like the good thief, had been forgiven.

Then, how her heart longed to be with her beloved, to spend her life in the loving arms of Jesus.

Some follow Jesus in distant lands; some serve him in big cities. Some find Jesus in the faces of the poor or the sick or the broken.

Thérèse longed to follow Jesus in the quiet of a holy house where women were free to love and serve him.

There was such a place in her town, where two of her sisters already lived. Thérèse wanted to join them, but she was only fifteen—just a girl. The bishop said she would have to wait.

So, she went to Rome. She visited the Colosseum and kissed the ground where martyrs died. She prayed that she, too, could be a martyr. And in her heart, she knew that her prayer would be answered.

Then with racing heart and high hopes she went to see the pope. She asked for permission to leave the world and live in the holy house.

But the pope did not say "yes." He only said, "If God wills it, it shall be so."

But that was not enough for Thérèse. On her knees before the pope, Thérèse begged and begged, until finally the Swiss guards picked her up and carried her away.

The road seemed blocked, as if Thérèse would never get her wish. She longed to enter the holy house, but the answer to her prayers seemed to be "no" —or at least "not yet."

But "yet" was not long in coming. Within a few months she left her home forever and entered the place of prayer to spend her life in joy and pain.

I am only a little flower, but in the arms of Jesus, I can love.

I am too small and weak to do the things I long for, but in the arms of Jesus I can love.

And my love will help those who cannot love.

Jesus will reach out through me to change lives and heal souls, to mend broken hearts and give meaning to those whose lives seem meaningless.

He asks me to join in his work, to join him in his joy, to join him in his sorrow, and in his suffering.

And I choose all.

The world is too busy to feel God's presence and to know his love. So most miracles take place in quiet ways, when the world is not paying attention.

A prayer reaches up to the throne of God, and the blind see, the sinner knows sorrow, and the lost are found.

At least that is the way it was in the life of Thérèse.

No one likes to suffer, to be sick with a headache or a fever, or to feel lost and alone, or to know that someone does not like you.

It is very hard to have others talk about us or laugh at us or ignore us. It is even harder to really love those who hurt us, and to want what is best for them. But that is what Thérèse did.

She used her pain as a prayer to help others. And so pain and suffering brought Thérèse closer and closer to Jesus, whose pain and suffering gives joy and peace and love to anyone who turns to him.

It is a mystery—something we do not understand—how God can take suffering and turn it into love and the power to heal broken hearts and wounded souls.

But Thérèse knew that this was true and she made her whole life a prayer for others, especially for priests who go to dangerous places to tell people about Jesus.

And in her pain and suffering she was filled with joy. She knew that she was too small to change the world and the lives of others, but that Jesus was changing the world and the lives of others through her pain and suffering.

The world is too busy to notice miracles, especially ones that happen in quiet houses of prayer.

And so the world took no notice of the quiet convent on a quiet street in Lisieux where a young woman was getting sicker and sicker, even as her love was getting stronger and stronger.

Years before on Christmas morning, Thérèse's pain was turned to joy and her love filled her house. Now in a more powerful way Thérèse's pain was turned to joy and her love filled the convent and began to spill over into the world.

Thérèse knew that Jesus loves us all and that because of his love he had been beaten and mocked, misjudged and hated, and cruelly put to death.

And so she joined Jesus in his pain because she was filled with love.

They put a bed next to a window that looked out on the garden, and Thérèse lay on the bed and saw the beauty of creation.

She was too sick to write and almost too sick to speak. She was only twenty-four years old and she was dying.

But Thérèse was happy.

Some dream of riches or fame and their lives are empty whether they get what they want or not. When pain comes they are angry. And when the end comes they feel empty and alone. They do not know that Jesus loves them, or they do not care.

And so they do not see the wonders he has been saving for them. They never know the joy of loving. But Thérèse could see those wonders and she knew how much Jesus loves those who do not love him.

And her great desire was to change hearts so that they could know the joy of God's love.

The world thinks heaven is a place to rest. But Thérèse knew that in heaven she could do much more than she could do on earth.

And she was eager to get busy.

And so before she died she said, "I will spend my heaven doing good on earth.

"I will let a shower of roses fall upon the earth."

And since then, God's Little Flower has been busy dropping spiritual roses to those who ask for her help.